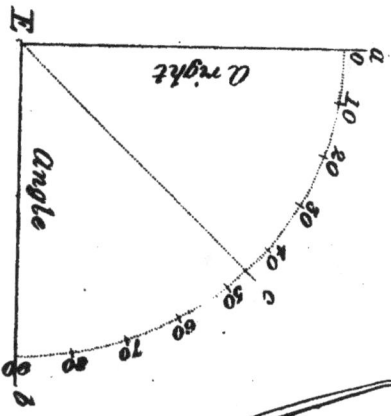

Angle

a right

0 10 20 30 40 50 60 70 80 90

c

I0169089

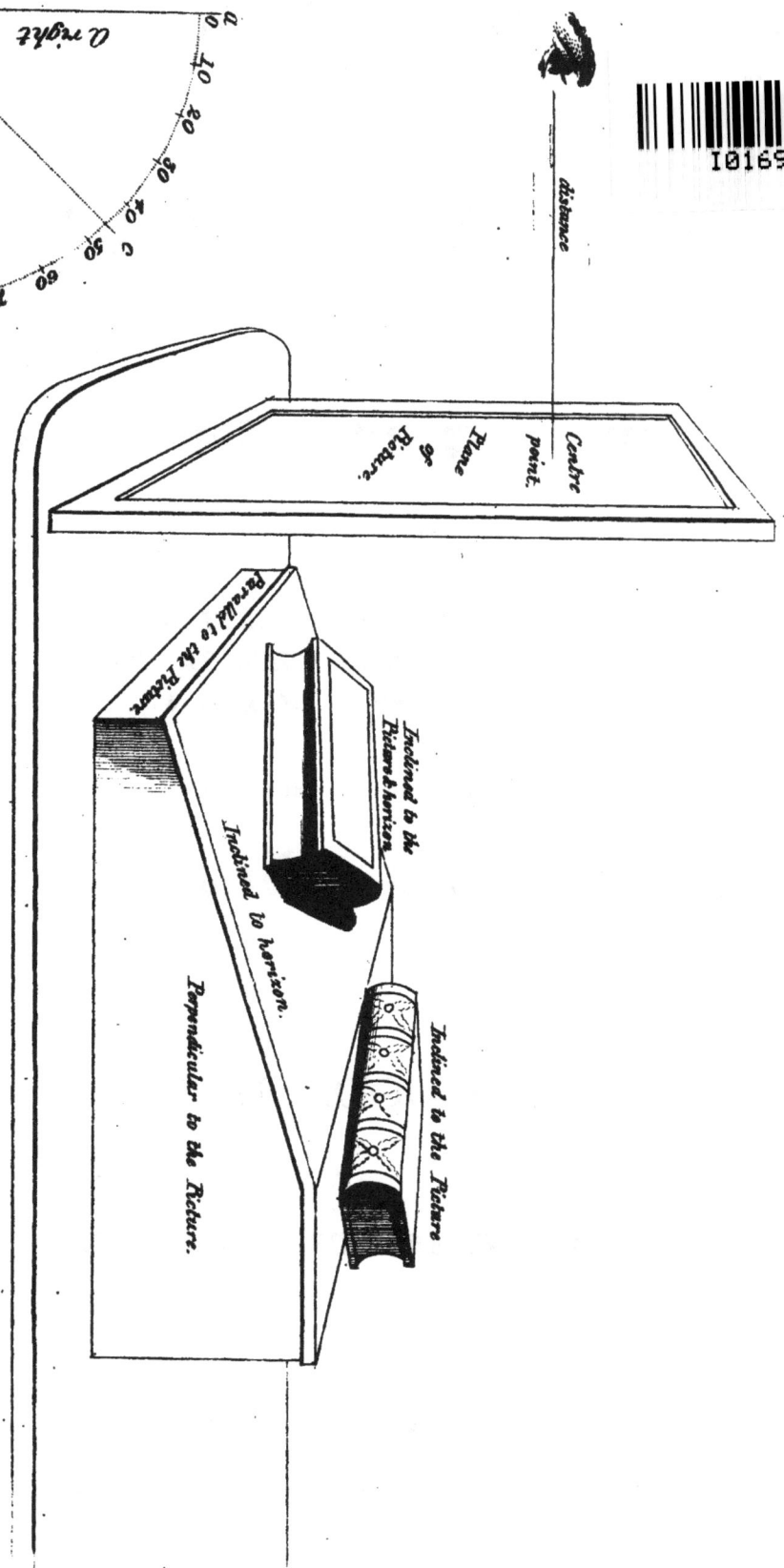

distance

Centre point.

Plane of Picture.

Parallel to the Picture

Inclined to the Picture & horizon

Inclined to horizon.

Inclined to the Picture

Perpendicular to the Picture.

Pl. 1.

A MANUAL

OF

PERSPECTIVE,

BEING A

Familiar Explanation of the Science,

INCLUDING THE

RULES NECESSARY FOR THE CORRECT REPRESENTATION
OF OBJECTS, THE PRINCIPLES OF SHADOWS,
REFLECTIONS IN WATER, &c.

ADAPTED MORE PARTICULARLY

FOR THE USE OF AMATEURS.

BY

J. WOOD, JUN.ᴿ

WITH NUMEROUS EXAMPLES.

WORCESTER:

PUBLISHED BY WOOD & SON, 35, FOREGATE-STREET.

1841.

INTRODUCTION.

THE voluminous nature of the majority of the works published on perspective has necessarily confined them to the possession of a few, and for this reason we so often see errors in the works of those who have made considerable progress in the art of drawing, and also of many who have attained even eminence in painting, which a knowledge of perspective would have enabled them to avoid; it is also for a similar reason that perspective has so generally acquired the character of an abstruse and difficult science, of which it is, to a great extent, if not altogether, undeserving. Of late years, however, many small works on the subject have been issued, but nearly the whole of them are either so full of technicalities as scarcely to be intelligible to the general reader, or else contain some fanciful method of their respective authors, which, although practically inferior to many others, yet, from their novelty, they have deemed worthy to lay before the public.

Perhaps the most desirable form of work on this subject, and one calculated to become the most generally useful, would be that in which the rudiments or first principles were concisely explained, divested as much as possible of technical terms, and illustrated with examples, according to the most approved methods of the best authors, of objects in the various positions in which they appear, the examples to be composed of the least complicated figures, and such as would prove the mathematical accuracy of the science.

Without pretending that the present little work possesses all these qualifications, it may be sufficient to state that such have been the aim of its author; how far he has succeeded it will be for his readers to determine.

WORCESTER, 1841.

MANUAL OF PERSPECTIVE.

PERSPECTIVE is founded principally on the fact that objects appear to diminish in size in proportion as their distance from the spectator is increased: for instance, if a long line of uniform objects be viewed at one end of the line, they will appear gradually to lessen, until, if continued to a great distance, the farthermost would appear a mere speck; or if a person stand looking along a straight road of considerable length, the opposite sides, as they recede from him, will appear gradually to approach each other, until they meet at a point in the extreme distance.

The principles by which these appearances are represented on a plane or flat surface, all parts of which are of necessity equally distant from the spectator, constitutes the science of perspective.

Some idea of the nature of the science may be obtained by supposing the surface upon which the picture is to be drawn transparent, and placed between the object and the spectator—so that the object could be seen distinctly through it : or, what would be the same thing, a person viewing an object through the glass of a window, by keeping himself perfectly steady (which he may do by fixing an eye-piece to look through at a certain distance from the glass), he may trace upon the glass an outline of the object, which would be (as far as regarded outline) a correct perspective representation of that object—every line of which would exactly correspond with a drawing made according to the rules of perspective on any opaque substance.

But perspective, in its strict sense, applies not only to the outline or shape of objects, but also to light, shade, and colour : the former has been distinguished by the term linear, and the latter by that of aeriel, but as it is to the linear that it is understood generally to apply, it may be sufficient here merely to notice the distinction.

In the practice of perspective, previously to commencing a drawing it is necessary to determine the situation of certain lines and points, and mark them on the paper, board, or whatever material be chosen. These are the horizontal and base lines, the centre of the picture, the vanishing points, and points of distance.

The horizontal line is a line drawn across the picture to indicate the level of the spectator's eye; it is the line upon which the vanishing points for all level or horizontal surfaces are situated: in sea views it is where the sea and sky appear to meet. Its situation in the drawing, if the spectator be supposed to stand on level ground, should be at about one-third its height; but if he stand on an eminence overlooking the object, it should be placed higher in proportion. It should always, however, be avoided to place it at exactly half the height of the drawing, as doing so would materially injure the effect of the best picture.

That part of the horizontal line which is immediately opposite the spectator, is called the centre of the picture, or point of sight. It is the vanishing point for the sides of all objects, and for all lines which recede from the spectator in a direction parallel to each other, and perpendicular to the picture. It indicates rather the centre of the spectator's field of view than the centre of the paper or canvass; and in most cases is better removed a little from the centre of the latter, as the representation thereby acquires more variety of form.

The distance at which the spectator is supposed to stand from the face or plane of the picture constitutes what is termed the distance of the picture (see plate 1.) The distance at which he stands is of course optional on the part of the spectator, but should nevertheless be proportioned in some degree to the size of the picture ; for instance, to see it conveniently, he should never stand at less than two-thirds the width of the picture distant from it ; if he stand nearer to it than this, the whole cannot come within the angle of his vision, and the objects in the drawing would appear distorted.   In practice, mark off on the horizontal line on each side of the centre point, a space equal to about two-thirds the width of the drawing, which will give the distance points—the use of which is to assist in determining the distance to which the perspective or receding sides of objects retire within the picture.

The base line is merely a line marking the lower edge of the picture, upon which the proper lengths and distances of the receding sides of objects are set down.

Rules for the perspective representation of objects in perhaps every position in which they can be placed, may be classed under the four following heads :—

1st. Parallel and perpendicular, in reference to the plane of the picture.

2nd. Inclined to the picture, or situated with one corner towards the spectator.

3rd. Inclined to the horizon, or, in other words, sloping.

4th. Inclined in reference both to the picture and to the horizon.

Plate 1 exhibits an example of each of these different positions. The front and upper portion of the top of the desk are parallel to the picture; the end forms a right angle with the front, and is therefore perpendicular to the picture; the word perpendicular being here used in reference to another line, and not in the sense of vertical, or perpendicular to the horizon. The desk is, then, in the first of the four positions we have named; the book resting on the upper flat part of it is in the second position; the sloping top of the desk will come under the third head; and the book resting upon it being in the same position as the other one, excepting that it lies on an inclined instead of a level surface, will exemplify the fourth position.

Plate 2, figure 1, shows the process for representing a cube and square plane in the first of these positions; B B there represents the base line of the drawing; v is the vanishing point, which, in the case of objects in this position, is identical with the centre of the picture; H H the horizontal line; and D D the points of distance. In commencing with the cube, the side which is parallel to the picture is first drawn perfectly square, and from its several angles the lines in the direction of v, which give the degree of diminution of its top and side; and to determine the distance to which these recede within the picture, the proper measurement of the side is marked on the base line from a to b, equal to $a\,c$; and a line drawn from b to the point of distance, the intersection of which with the vanishing line from a to v will give the perspective extent of that side of the cube, at which point the vertical line is raised, and from the point where it intersects the upper vanishing line, a line drawn parallel to the horizontal line will complete the cube.

The situation of the square plane differs from that of the cube in being situated within the picture; therefore, after having drawn the vanishing lines $d\,e$ to v, instead of setting off the extent of its receding side on the base line, first mark off the distance at which it is situated within the picture from e to f, and then the extent of the side from f to g, from which points lines to the point D will give the perspective situation of the plane.

The line from g to the distance point might have been dispensed with, as the line from f to D, crossing, as it does (in a diagonal direction), the square, is sufficient; but it is here inserted, because if the figure had been any other than a square, it would have been absolutely necessary.

If the whole of figure 1 were drawn on an enlarged scale upon glass, instead of on paper, and a cube and square plane of wood or other material, of a size corres-

Pl.2

Fig. 1

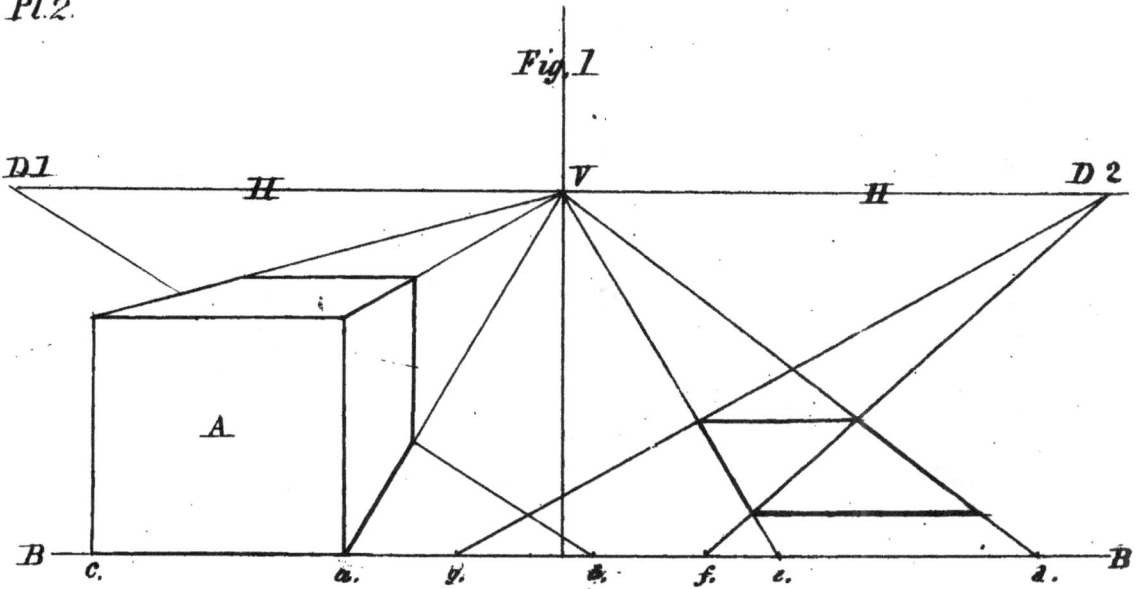

Fig. 2

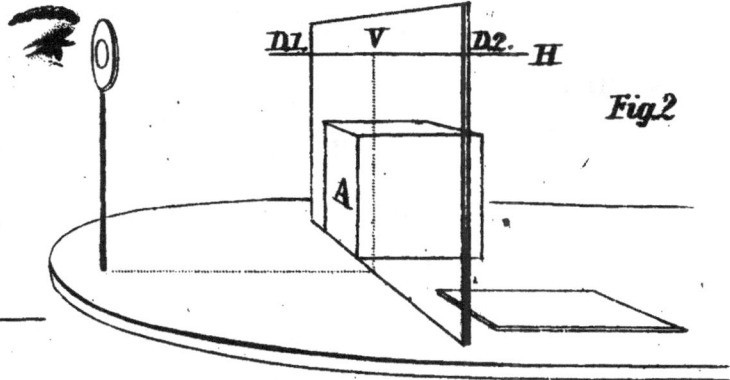

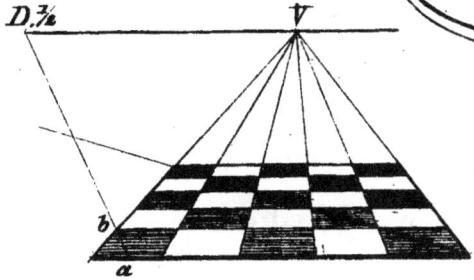

Fig. 3

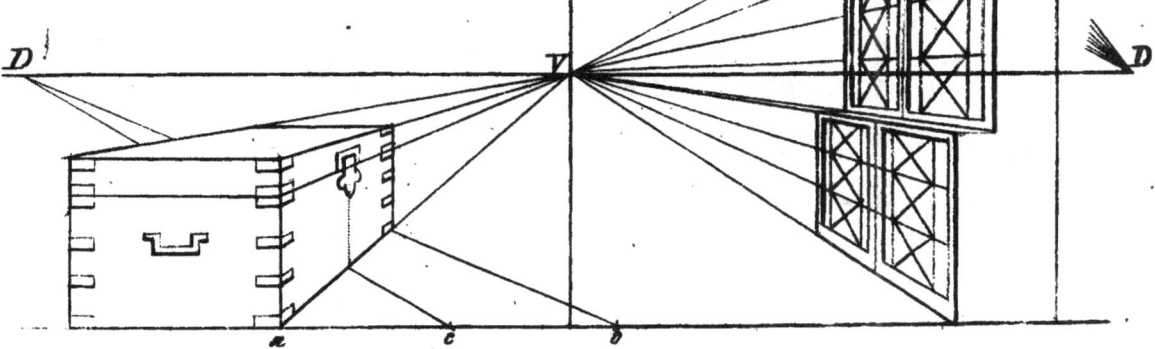

ponding with the representation on the glass, were placed behind it in the way represented in figure 2, the glass resting edgewise on the table, and in contact with the face A of the cube, by fixing a piece of card with a hole in it, as an eye-piece, opposite to the point v, and at a distance from it equal to that of either of the distance points, upon looking through the eye-piece, the spectator would see that the objects themselves exactly corresponded with the various lines of the drawing on the glass, filling up the outline to the greatest nicety—thus proving the correctness of the principles upon which perspective is founded.

It may be observed that the eye-piece may be placed at any distance thought proper from the glass, provided that the points D D be placed at a corresponding distance from the centre or vanishing point.

The box in figure 3 is put in perspective in the same way as the cube; in order to find the centre of the front, from the centre of the space *a b*, which is the proportion of length to the breadth, or end of the box, draw a line to the point of distance, and from the point where it intersects the lower vanishing line, raise a vertical line, which will give the place for the lock, which serves to indicate the centre.

In the example of the bookcase, instead of the various measurements being set down on the base line,

they are marked on a line drawn from the top of the
object in a direction parallel to the horizontal line, and
give the perspective proportions on the upper vanishing
line of the front; this method may be adopted when
the base of the object is concealed from view by the
interposition of some other object.

For the convenience of having the distance points
within the compass of the drawing, the method shewn
in figure 4 may oftentimes be practised. After the lines
to the vanishing point are inserted, a line is drawn
from the centre a of the left-hand square in the direction of $D\frac{1}{2}$, which latter point is situated at half the
distance of the spectator from v; from the point at
which this line intersects the left-hand vanishing line,
a line drawn horizontally completes the first row of
squares. To ascertain the extent of the other rows, a
line is drawn diagonally through the right-hand square,
and continued across all the vanishing lines, at the
intersection of which with each, lines drawn parallel to
the first complete the figure.

In representing an interior, the shape of the drawing
should be first proportioned to the subject; then the
horizontal line should be inserted at its proper height,
or at such height as to be on a level with the eye of
a figure, if one were represented in the picture; the
vanishing point should be rather nearer one side of the

drawing than the other, and each distance point at about two-thirds the width of the drawing distant from that point.

After having drawn the various vanishing lines, the first thing will be to determine the length of the room, which is done by setting down its measurement on the base line, and carrying a line to the point of distance. But before doing so, it may be observed that the full length of an interior should never be represented, for the spectator, standing as he must within the room, cannot see at the same view all the parts immediately adjacent to him; a representation of its full length would therefore appear disproportionably long when compared with the real room.

Of the space to be deducted, let the spectator, when standing at one end, mark the distance at which he stands from the nearest side wall, and deduct the same from the length of the room; then commence the drawing with those parts which are situated at that distance from the end at which he is standing.

In the example, plate 3, figure 1, which represents a room with three windows, the first pier and part of the first window are left out of the drawing; the widths of the other piers and windows are marked on the base line, and lines drawn from them to D, which, where they cross the lower vanishing line of that side of the room, give the situations of the windows, and also that of one of the furthermost angles of the room; the general form of the room may then be completed by drawing lines, as in the example.

To put circles in perspective it is necessary first to describe one with the compasses of the size required, then to enclose it in a square, and draw lines across it, as in the accompanying figure, which intersect each other at eight different points in the circumference of the circle; then put the square with its enclosed lines in perspective, according to the rules given for figure 1, plate 1, and draw the circle by means of the hand through the eight different points.

The same principle applied to arches, is represented in figure 3; A is the proportion of the arch when viewed in front, which is first drawn by means of compasses, and then enclosed and intersected by right lines, giving the points *a b c*; the points *d* are then marked on the vertical line B T, and lines drawn from them to V; the full width of the arch A must be marked on the base line, commencing at B; then the width of the pier, then the arch again, and so on according to the number to be put into perspective; from which marks, lines to the point D will give the perspective width of the arches and piers at the points where they intersect the lower vanishing line; from which points the vertical lines form-

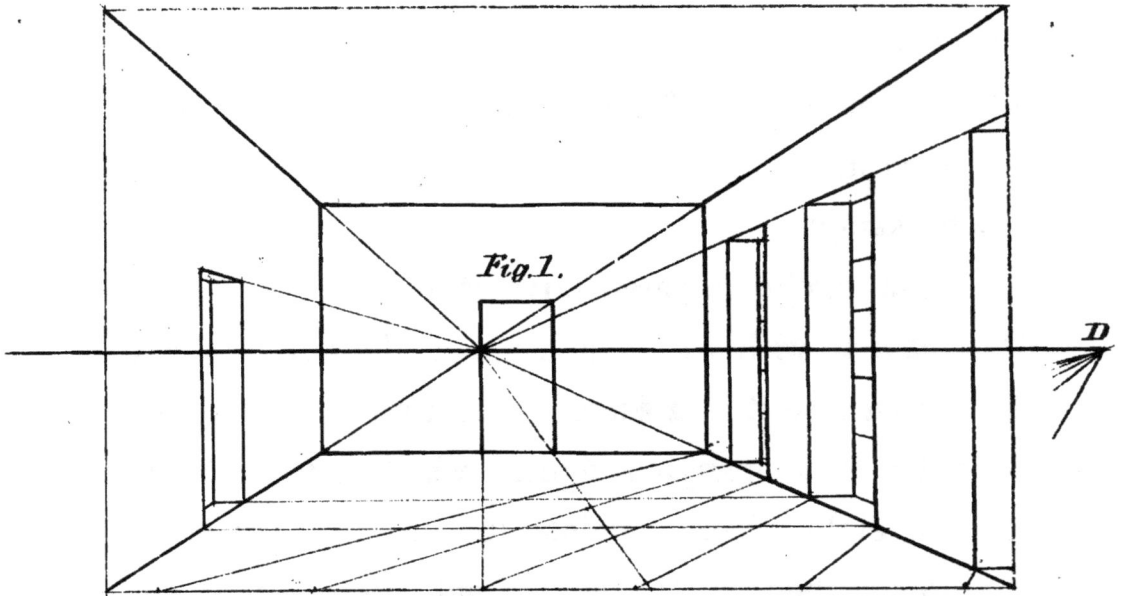

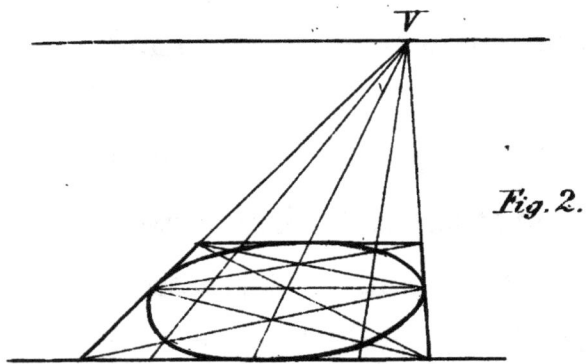

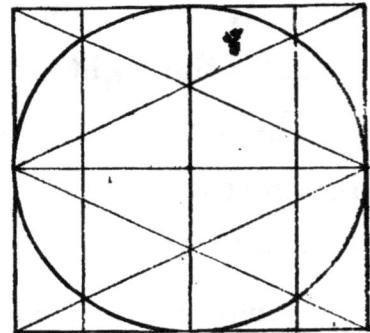

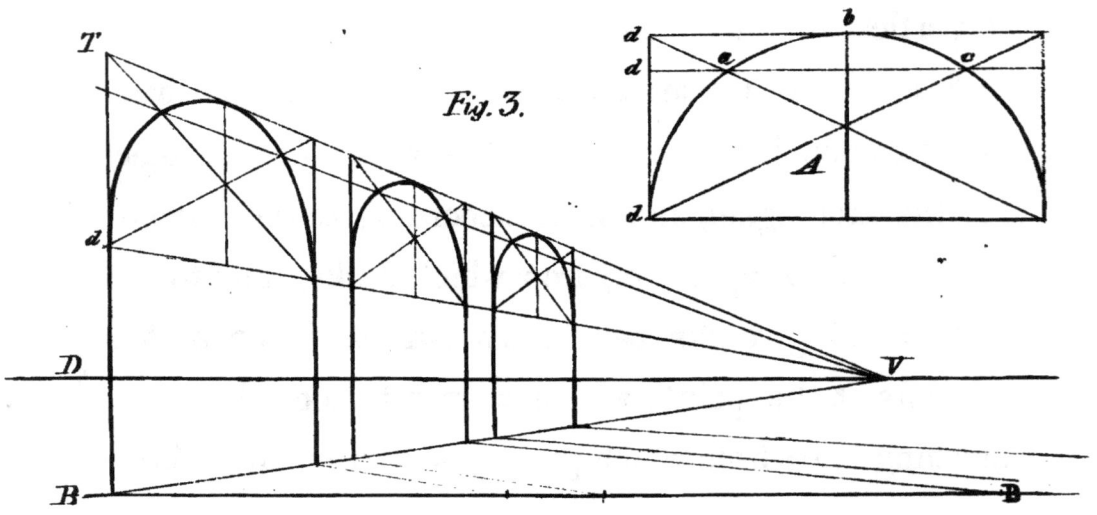

Pl. 3.

Fig. 1.

D

V

Fig. 2.

Fig. 3.

T

d

D

B

b

d

d

d

a

c

A

d

V

B

ing the piers are raised, and the perspective centre of each arch found by means of the cross lines, termed diagonals, a vertical line drawn through which gives the point *b*. We have now the points *a b c* in each division as guides whereby to draw the arches.

OF OBJECTS INCLINED TO THE PICTURE.

The sides of objects we have hitherto considered have been situated in a parallel and perpendicular direction to the plane of the picture, and have required but one vanishing point. If we now suppose the object turned so that one corner shall be towards the spectator, the sides of it receding from him, it will require two vanishing points, the sides which before were parallel being now inclined to the picture. And if the sides be inclined in an equal degree, the angle of inclination is said to be 45 degrees,* which is halfway between perpendicular and parallel; in which case, the distance points for objects in the former position become vanish-

---

* For the measuring of angles the circle is understood to be divided into 360 parts, called degrees, and the angle which one line forms with another (the point of their intersection being placed at the centre of the circle) is described as occupying so many of those degrees. Thus, in plate 1, figure 2, the line *b* forms with *a* an angle of 90 degrees, being one quarter of the circle: the line *c* an angle of 45 degrees, and so on for any intermediate angle.

ing points. This is exemplified in plate 4, figure 1, where the points D 1 and D 2 are distance points for the figure of the square plane, but vanishing points for the lines which cross in a diagonal direction its centre; and also in figure 2, where the square plane is turned, so that it forms the above angle of 45 degrees with the plane of the picture, and its sides, or edges, are therefore in a situation parallel to the diagonals in figure 1; when thus turned its diagonals fall, the one perpendicular and the other parallel to the plane of the picture.

In figure 2 these points are marked v 1 and v 2, and the distance points D 1 and D 2; the latter, it will be remembered, represent the distance of the spectator from the vanishing points, neither of which are any longer identical with the centre of the picture, from which point the distance has in all the previous examples been measured. In this position they are found by first setting off the distance at which the spectator stands from c to E, which, in the case of objects situated at this particular angle, would be equal to the distance from c to either of the vanishing points; then the lines from E to the vanishing points are drawn, and the lengths of those lines transferred to the horizontal line, giving the points D 1 and D 2.

It need scarcely be observed that the true position of the line c E would be projecting from c out in

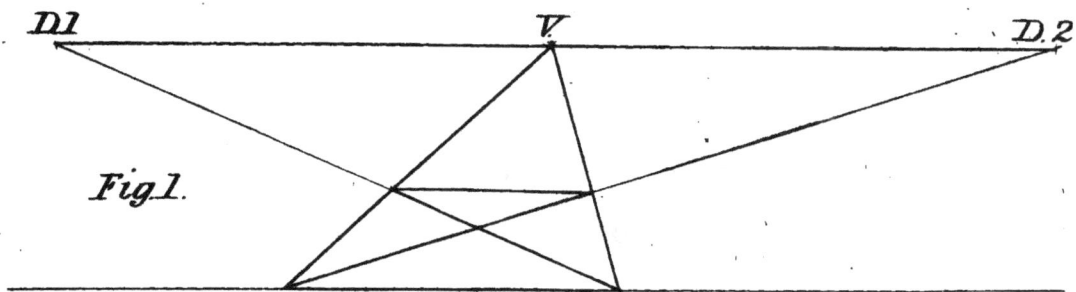

Fig. 1.

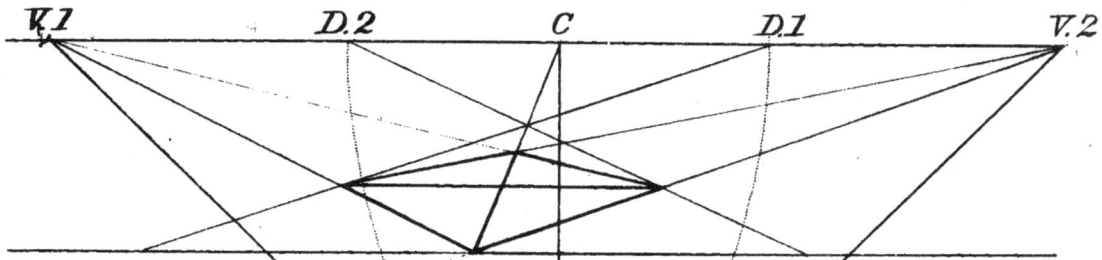

Fig. 2.

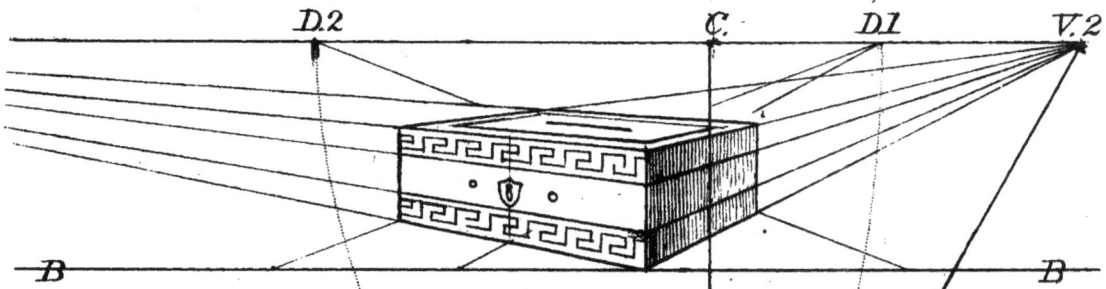

Fig. 3.

front of the picture, in a direction perpendicular 'to its surface, at the extreme end of which, namely E, the spectator's eye is supposed to be situated, viewing the object; it therefore represents the direct line of his vision transferred, for the convenience of practice, to the surface of the drawing. It might be set off either above or below the horizontal line, but the latter is generally more convenient, as it does not occupy so much space as the former would.

The line P P is called the parallel of the picture; it serves as a guide from which to set off the lines by which the vanishing points are found, when the precise angle which the object forms with the picture is given. In the example, these lines are situated at an angle of 45 degrees with the line P P, the same as that which the square plane forms with the base line of the picture, although in appearance the latter is considerably less in consequence of being seen in an oblique direction.

But, as before observed, it is only when the object is inclined to the picture at this particular angle, that the distance points for objects in the first position become vanishing points; if the degree of inclination exceed or fall short of 45 degrees, then the vanishing points may be found, as exemplified in figure 3, where the front of the box is more inclined to parallel than to perpendicular, and the end, on the contrary, more to the latter than the former. After having fixed the base and horizontal lines, and the distance of the spectator, on the line c e, commence by drawing the upright corner of the box; then the lower vanishing line of the front, at any inclination thought proper; continue the latter by means of a rule until it intersects the horizontal line at v 1, to which point draw the various converging lines of the front and top; then draw the line from v 1 to e, and, forming a right angle with it, the line from e to v 2, by which means the latter point is found. The distance points are found, as in the previous example, by transferring the lengths of the lines e v 1 and e v 2 to the horizontal line, as indicated by the dotted curved lines.

The length and breadth of the box may then be set off on the base line on each side of the vertical line, which forms the corner; and lines drawn in the direction of the points of distance will give the perspective measurements* of those parts, from which points vertical

---

* The word measurement is not here, as it is in many works on this subject, intended to denote feet and inches, as these can be useful only to the architectural or mechanical draughtsman: the amateur need only proportion the different parts by eye; for instance, if the length of the real box be double that of its height, mark off on the base line a space equal to double the height of the nearest corner of the box, and the same of the breadth.

lines raised will complete the outline of the front and end ; the top may then be completed by drawing lines from the tops of these two vertical lines to the vanishing points.

These examples will be found sufficient for the delineation of most rectangular objects ; the circle, arches, and other curved figures must, as they are in parallel and perpendicular perspective, be enclosed by angular figures, and intersected by lines at certain points in their circumference, and the perspective position of the points found in the manner there directed—the only variation being in the situation of the vanishing and distance points of the angular figure by which it is encompassed.

OF OBJECTS INCLINED TO THE HORIZON.

In this position it is necessary that the vanishing point be removed from the horizontal line (in some part of which it has hitherto always been situated), and placed on a vertical line, at a distance above the horizontal line, proportioned to the degree of inclination of the object. The principal thing is to determine the height at which to place the vanishing point, which is done by the following process.

In figure 1, plate 5, the front of the house is perpendicular to the picture, and consequently would vanish at the centre point; the distance of the spectator is at D 1, from which point a line is set off, forming, with the horizontal line, the same degree of inclination as the roof of the original building, and where this intersects the vertical line previously drawn through the central vanishing point, is the vanishing point for the nearest sloping sides of the roof; the height of the roof may be ascertained either by finding the centre, or apex, by means of the diagonal lines, as represented in the first division of the house, or by placing a vanishing point on the vertical line at the same distance below the horizontal line as the one above, and drawing the furthermost sides of the roof to it.

The inclination of the flight of steps is not so great as that of the roof; therefore the line representing it, and which commences at D 2, intersects the vertical nearer to the horizontal line than that does which represents the inclination of the roofs.

The representation of uphill and downhill views is the same in principle as that of objects inclined to the horizon. In the first of these, the ground being raised towards the eye, the boundary lines, instead of converging to a vanishing point on the horizontal line, as they would if it were level, will meet at a point at a

Pl. 5.

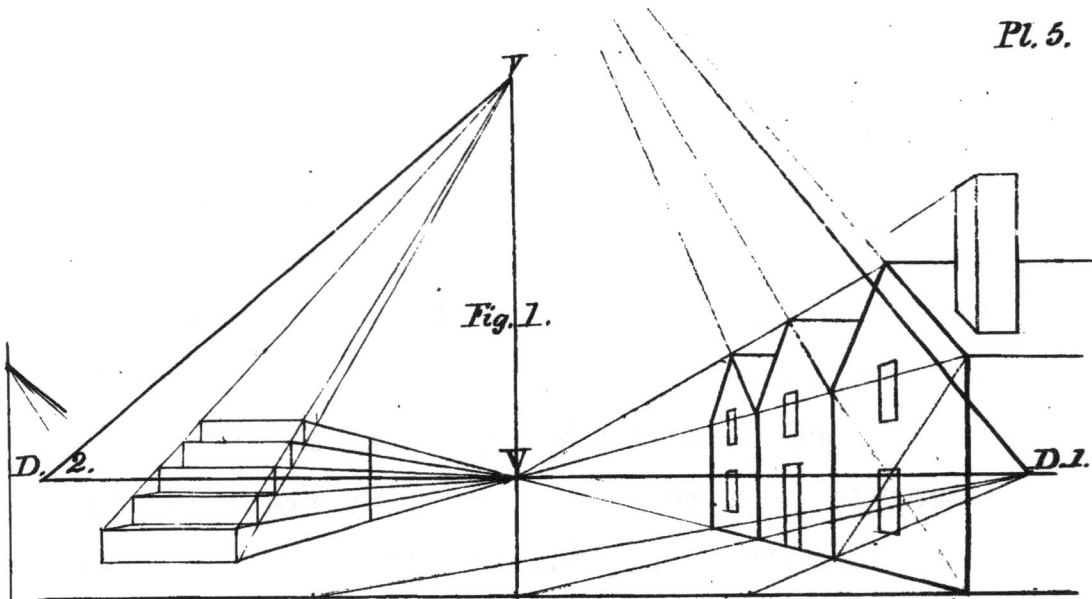

Fig. 1.

D. 2.

D. 1.

V.

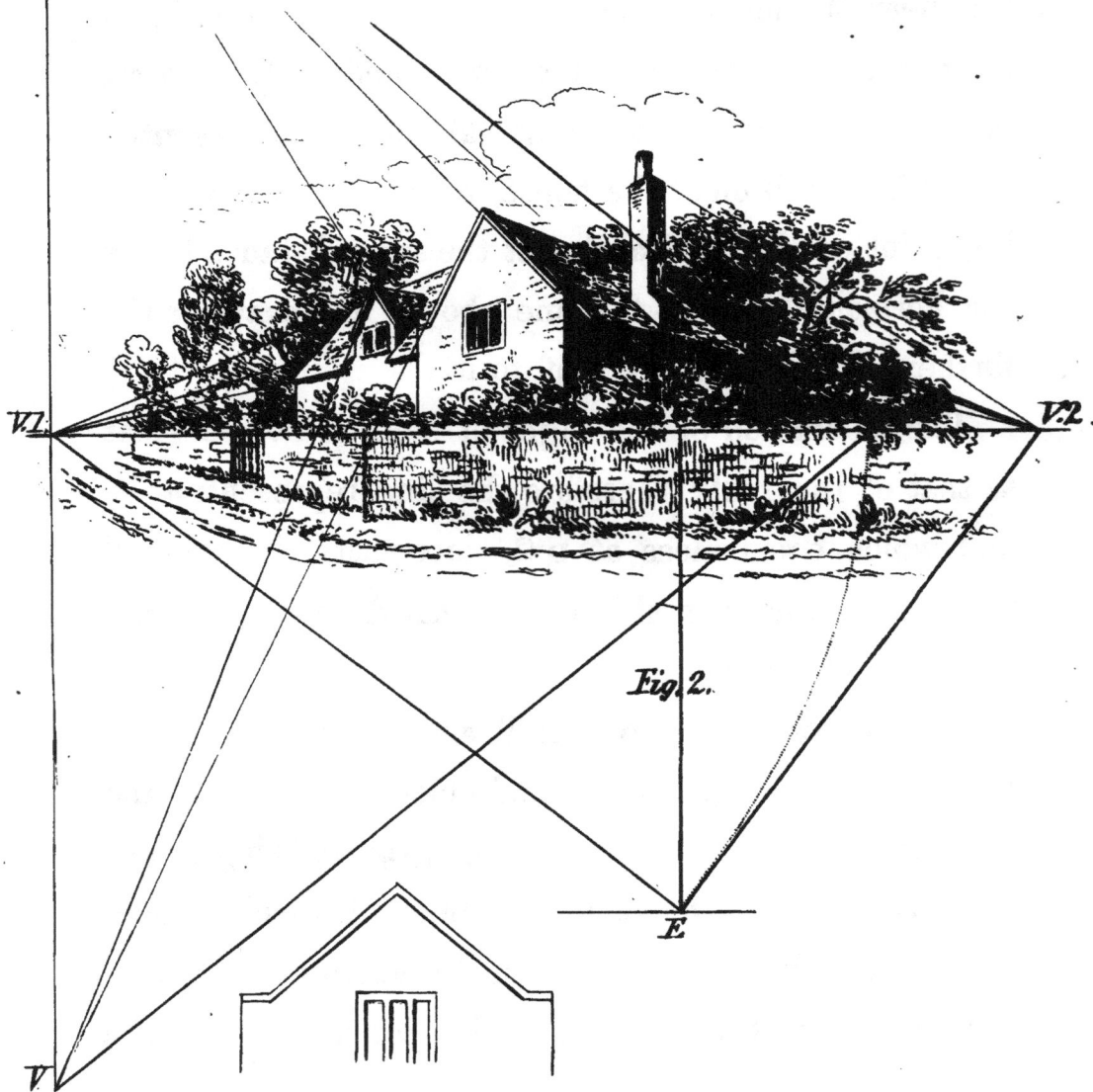

V.1.

V.2.

Fig. 2.

E

V.

distance above that line proportioned to the steepness of the hill. In the downhill view the converging lines, which in a road include the hedges, footpaths, and markings of wheels, will, on the contrary, have their vanishing point below the horizontal line ; but the vanishing lines of buildings, in both instances, still converge to the horizontal line. In cases where the hill is very steep, the ground itself is frequently lost sight of; the effect of a distant view taken from its summit can then only be produced by the partial introduction of buildings or of figures, more or less of the parts of which will be visible over the ridge, according as they happen to be situated higher or lower on the hill.

OF OBJECTS INCLINED TO THE PICTURE AND HORIZON.

In what we have termed the fourth position, the object is inclined to the picture as well as to the horizon, as exemplified in plate 1, in the drawing of the book situated on the inclined part of the desk, with one corner towards the picture ; and also in plate 5, figure 2, the roof and gable ends of the building being examples of this position. The point E in the latter example is the relative position of the spectator in front of c ; v 1 and v 2 are the vanishing points; D 1 is one of the distance points, and is distant from v 1 equal to the length of the line E v 1; from this point the lines which represent the inclination of the roof are set off above and below the horizontal line; and at the intersections which they form with the vertical line drawn through the point v 1, are the vanishing points required.

Thus the process for representing objects in this position is very similar to the last; indeed, it does not consist so much in any variation in the process as it does in merely changing the position of some of the lines; for instance, the lines representing the inclination of the roofs are commenced in both at the distance of the spectator from the vanishing point of that side of the object on which the slope occurs, and the vertical line which they are made to intersect is in both raised through the latter vanishing point. So that the main difference resulting is from the change in the situation of the vanishing and distance points, as explained in the first and second positions.

In sketching from the real object, or in making drawings in which extraordinary correctness is not required, the line showing the degree of inclination of the original may be dispensed with. In such cases the eye may be depended upon for the correctness of one line of the inclined object; for instance, the line b, in the example figure 1, the required vanishing point being at its point of intersection with the vertical line.

OF SHADOWS.

Shadows are of two kinds—those caused by natural, and those by artificial light; the former by the sun or moon, and the latter by lamps, candles, &c. In consequence of the magnitude and great distance of the sun, it has been laid down as a rule that upon our earth its rays fall parallel to each other; therefore a shadow projected by a vertical straight-sided object would be contained within two parallel lines. The practice is founded upon this principle: in plate 6, figure 1, the direction of the shadows is represented by merely drawing lines from the bases of the objects parallel to the base line of the picture, and their lengths determined by drawing other lines from the upper angles parallel to each other, and at the same degree of inclination that the sun's rays are supposed to make with the horizon, which give the proper lengths at their points of intersection. In this case the sun is supposed to be even with, or the term is, in the plane of the picture.

In cases, which are more frequent, of the sun being situated either in front or behind the picture,

and the shadows consequently projected from or towards
the spectator, although the shadows lie, as in the
first case, in reality parallel to each other, yet, according as they either approach or retire from the spectator,
they will appear to him (in accordance with the principle of the diminution of objects by distance), either
as diverging from, or converging to, a point.   In the
case of objects situated on level ground, this point is
always situated on the horizontal line, and immediately
under the sun; it has, therefore, sometimes been called
the seat of the sun on the horizon.

In practice, first fix the position of the sun, and by
drawing a line from it perpendicular to the horizontal
line, ascertain the vanishing point for the shadows,
figure 2. The lines ruled from the point s intersecting
the bases of the upright sticks, are first drawn of any
indefinite length; then, by means of the lines drawn
from s 2 through the tops of the sticks, the lengths of
the shadows are determined.

When the shadows are cast from the spectator, the
situation of the sun is of course in front of the picture,
and behind the spectator; in practice it must be set off
below the horizontal line, and the vanishing point for
the shadows marked on that line, as in figure 3.   Lines
being drawn from the point marked sun, to the
upper angles of the objects, will, at the points where

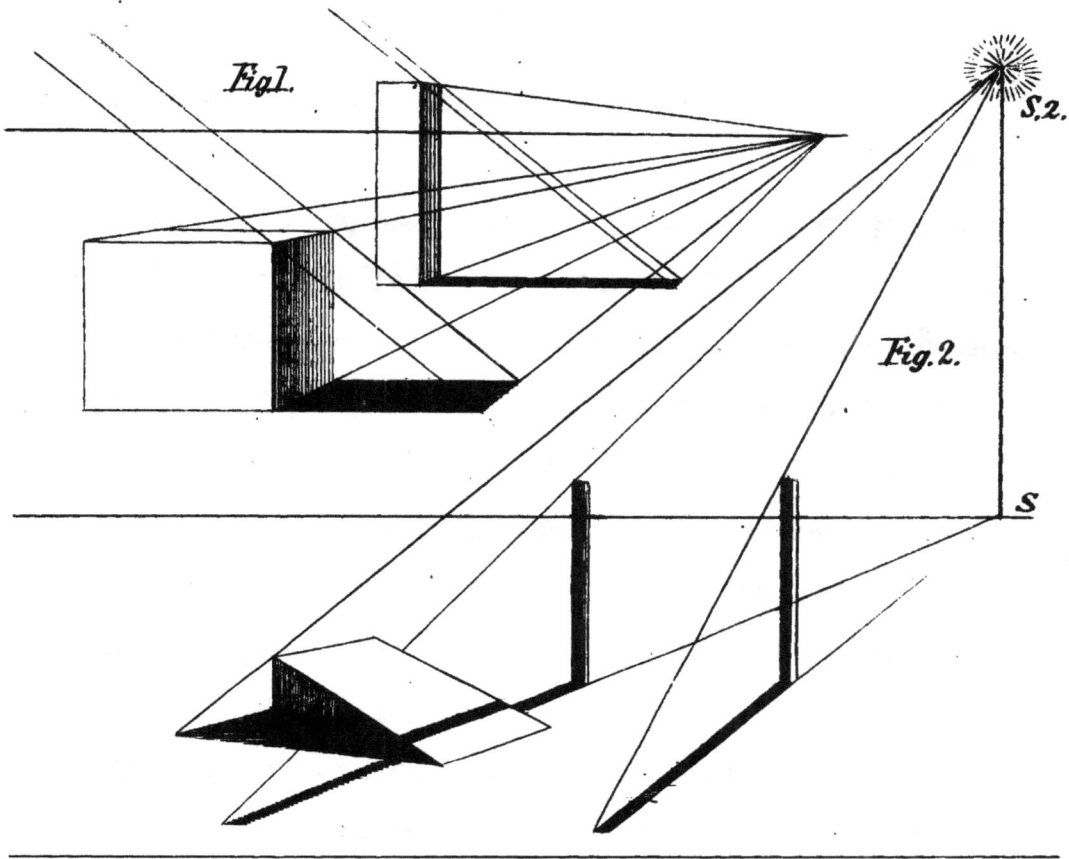

_Pl.6._

Fig.1.

Fig.2.

_S.2._

_s_

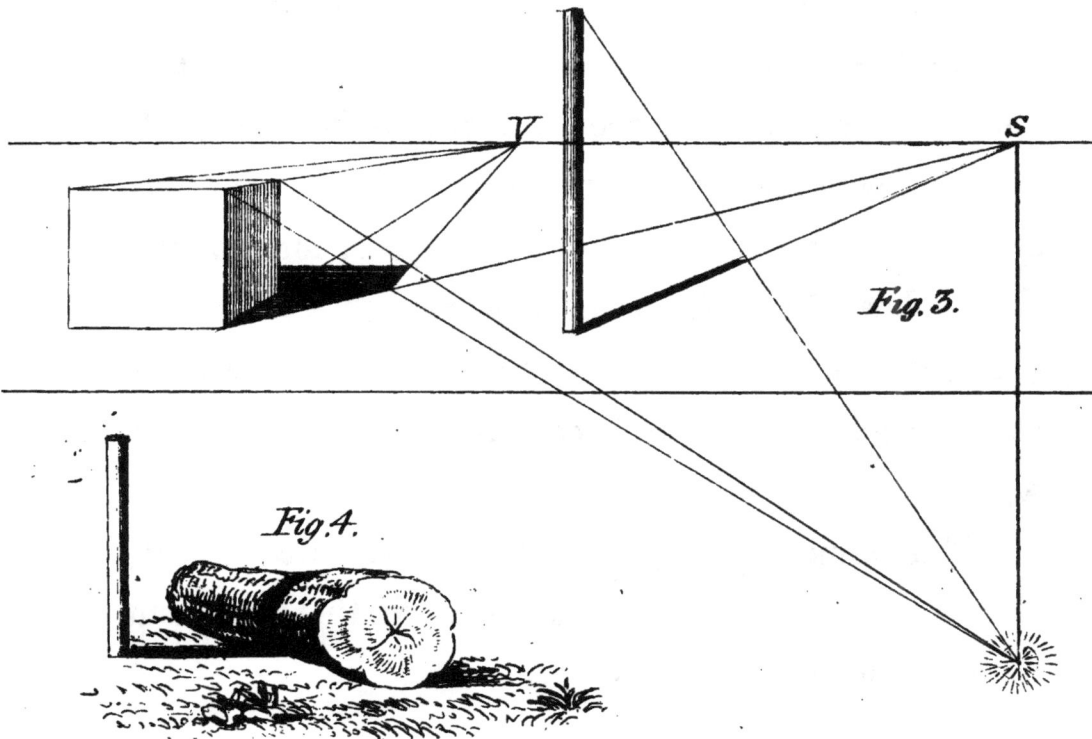

_V_   _s_

Fig.3.

Fig.4.

they intersect the shadows, determine their respective lengths.

It may be observed in these examples—and it is necessary clearly to understand—that the vanishing point for shadows is altogether distinct from any vanishing point used in the delineation of the object, its position being dependent on that of the sun.

In the case of a shadow cast on a round body, or a body of any form differing from a plane, the shadow will assume the form of that body, as exemplified in figure 4.

The principal difference between natural and artificial light is, that in the latter case, instead of the light proceeding in parallel rays from a large body at a great distance, it radiates from a small centre of light situated comparatively close to, or amongst, the objects it illumines; therefore the shadows, instead of being capable of being contained within two parallel lines, would increase in width from the base of the object; for instance, the shadow of a book placed edgewise on a table, at a short distance from a candle, would be of the same width as the book only where it commenced close to it, and would gradually increase in width to its remote end; but if illumined by the sun, as we have already seen, the shadow would be of the same width throughout its entire length.

In plate 7, figure 1, first ascertain the point s on the floor, by drawing a line from the light perpendicular to the floor; from this point draw along the floor lines intersecting the legs of the table, and then the rays from the candle, intersecting the four corners of the table, to the lines previously drawn along the floor, at which points the shadow will terminate; then, to complete the outline of it, connect the points thus found by straight lines.

For the shadow of the screen draw lines from s to the wall through the lower angles of the screen, and from the points where they reach the wall, raise two perpendicular lines; the height of the shadow is determined by lines drawn direct from the light through the upper angles of the screen.

For the beam projecting from the wall it is necessary first to find on the wall a vanishing point for its shadow, answering to the point s on the floor; this is done by first drawing a line from s to the wall, from thence a perpendicular up the wall, and a line horizontally from the light to the wall, which will give the point s2; then represent the shadow in the way shown in the example.

For any object projecting from the ceiling or the opposite wall, a vanishing point for the shadow would be required on the same, and may be found by a similar process.

Pl.7.

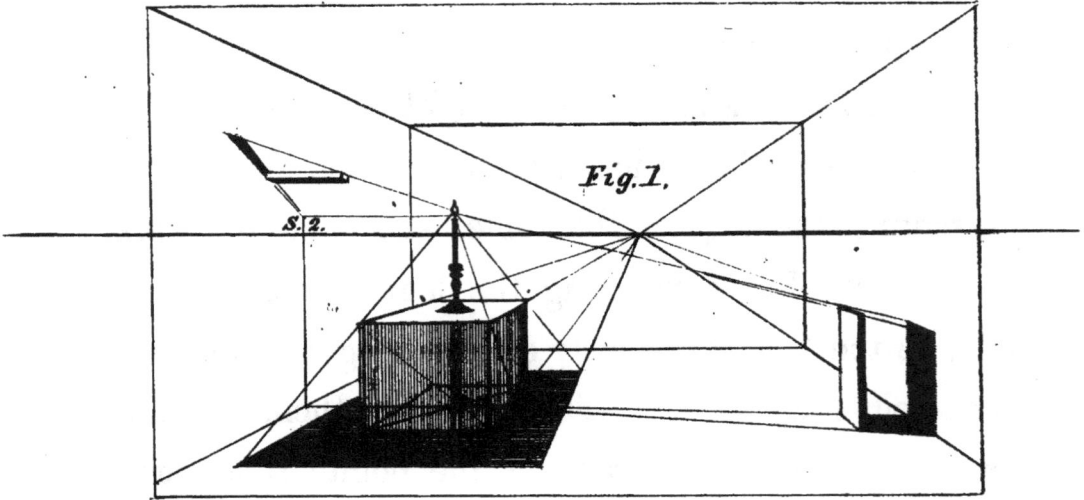

Fig.1.

S.2.

Fig.2.

Fig.3.

It may be as well to observe that shadows should never terminate so harshly at their boundaries as possibly may be inferred from these rules; a shadow should always terminate gradually with what is termed a penumbra or half shadow, forming a connecting link between it and the light beyond; it should ever be borne in mind that in the representation of shadows they should never convey the idea of substance.

OF REFLECTIONS IN WATER.

This part of our subject is very simple; there are few who have not observed that the reflection of any object in still water is always an exact but an inverted image of the object itself; therefore, when, as in figure 2, plate 7, the object is situated rising immediately from the water, no other rule is required to represent its reflection; but if, as in figures 3 and 4, it be situated on a bank at some distance from the water's edge, the eye must judge of the level at which the water would be (if it extended so far) perpendicularly below the building; then the height of the building, together with the space between its base and the water-mark, which is indicated in figures 3 and 4 by the dotted line, are to be inverted below that line. But we may observe of reflections generally that a perfect inverted image of

any object can be reflected only when the water is
perfectly still; if its surface be agitated by the wind,
or any other cause, it will reflect only, and that in a
very confused manner, the bases of those objects which
rise immediately from its surface, and as this must be
oftentimes the case, strict adherence to rules is seldom
required in the delineation of reflections.

THE END.

WORCESTER:
PRINTED BY CHALK AND HOLL, HERALD-OFFICE.

www.ingramcontent.com/pod-product-compliance
Lightning Source LLC
Chambersburg PA
CBHW081453070426
42452CB00042B/2687